# Barbie™

# Fashion Icon

Illustrations by
Alessandra Scandella

LAURENCE KING

LAURENCE KING

First published in Italy in 2024 by 24 ORE
Cultura S.r.l., Milan

This edition published in Great Britain and the
United States in 2025 by Laurence King

Graphic Design and Layout by Pepe Nymi
Illustrations by Alessandra Scandella
Translation from the Italian by Nanette McGuinness

 A CIP catalogue record for this book is
available from the British Library.

ISBN: 978-1-510-23237-2

10 9 8 7 6 5 4 3 2 1

Printed in China

MIX
Paper | Supporting
responsible forestry
FSC® C020056
FSC
www.fsc.org

Laurence King
An imprint of
Hachette Children's Group
Part of Hodder and Stoughton Limited
Carmelite House
50 Victoria Embankment
London EC4Y 0DZ

An Hachette UK Company
www.hachette.co.uk
www.hachettechildrens.co.uk
www.laurenceking.com

The authorised representative in the EEA is Hachette Ireland,
8 Castlecourt Centre, Dublin 15, D15 XTP3, Ireland
(email: info@hbgi.ie)

1959

# Teenage Fashion Model Barbie

**PROFESSION:** MODEL

**STYLE:** MOVIE ICON

**SPECIAL FEATURES:** REMOVABLE SUNGLASSES

**ICONIC ELEMENT:** BLACK-AND-WHITE STRIPED SWIMSUIT

**SIGNIFICANCE:** THE FIRST BARBIE IN HISTORY

**INSPIRATION:** 1950s MOVIE STAR

Barbara Millicent Roberts, a model from Willows, Wisconsin, made her debut at the New York Toy Fair on March 9, 1959. From that day on, the toy world would never be the same. Created by designer Ruth Handler, *Teenage Fashion Model Barbie* was fundamentally different from other children's dolls of the time. She didn't have the features of a chubby little girl wearing Victorian clothing or even a baby in swaddling clothes. Instead, standing 11.5 inches tall,

## 1959

she encapsulated the features of a 1950s movie star. From the moment of her debut, it was clear that Barbie was connected to fashion, lifestyle, and modernity in a way that no other doll had ever been and probably ever will be. With her teased-out blond ponytail, elegant makeup, black sunglasses, and black-and-white striped swimsuit, *Teenage Fashion Model Barbie* was the latest in fashion. Indeed, Lycra fabric—which revolutionized not just swimwear but, above all, the daily lives of women worldwide, too—had been invented just a year earlier. The first Barbie had an amazing impact. In 1959 alone, 351,000 Barbies entered the homes of just as many American children. It was the debut of an icon that, for generations of young women, would be synonymous with fashion as well as creativity, imagination, and personal expression.

**FUN FACT:** In 1959, Barbie sold for $3 (USD) ... Today, in good condition, this doll is worth over $20,000 (USD) on the antique market.

# Glasses

**ICONIC FEATURE:** THE FIRST BARBIE'S CAT-EYE GLASSES

**SIGNIFICANCE:** A TRIP THROUGH THE HISTORY OF DESIGN FROM THE 1950S TO TODAY

The link between Barbie and sunglasses happened right away. The first model in 1959 wore gorgeous cat-eye sunglasses with white frames and clear, light-blue lenses. Over the course of Barbie's existence, her designers created likely one of the biggest collections of sunglasses in the fashion world, a collection rivaling those of Iris Apfel or Lina Wertmüller, two famous icons who made unique, extravagant glasses their signature accessories and owned hundreds of pairs of them. To look more charismatic and mysterious, or just to protect her from the sun, Barbie very often had a pair of sunglasses as an accessory to finish her "glamour look" and accompany her to many different events.

But glasses weren't merely simple accessories that adorned her face. They were also an element that illustrated her outdoorsy life,one filled with ever-new adventures.

**FUN FACT:** Since the release of the *Barbie* movie, several brands have introduced men's and women's glasses inspired by the ones worn by the actors in the film. these, in turn, were based on glasses that Barbie and Ken have worn over the years.

## 1959

# Commuter Set Barbie

**STYLE:** SOPHISTICATED ELEGANCE

**INSPIRATION:** MODERN CAREER WOMEN

New York, Grand Central Station, 9 a.m.: the constant noise of heels on the marble floor and a strong feeling of purpose in the air. Millions of women step off the train to go to work, get to the heart of the city, build careers, and earn a living. They're commuters, daily travelers, women on the move. The essence of Barbie's dynamic energy was contained in the commuter set that rounded out her first wardrobe.

The elegant, sober look was a big classic in the late '50s. It featured a navy blue collarless jacket (à la Chanel), a pencil skirt in the same color, a light blue checked shirt for day wear, and a bodysuit in white satin for the evening look.

# 1959

The accessories exuded the everyday elegance of the time: a two-strand crystal necklace and matching bracelet, a round red hatbox, and a hat with silk flowers. This outfit made a clear statement that laid the foundation for Barbie's story and over 250 careers: she leads a dynamic, active, independent life. For girls of the time, Barbie was a constructive role model. She let them imagine a lifestyle beyond stereotypes that only saw women as homemakers, and flung open the doors to the future.

# Hairstyle

**ICONIC FEATURE:**
PONYTAIL

**SIGNIFICANCE:** A STYLE REFLECTING ERAS OF THE 20$^{TH}$ CENTURY

Together with her outfit, makeup, and features, Barbie's hairstyle mirrored the major cultural changes in society during the second half of the 20th century. Among the different hairdos the doll has sported over the years, the ponytail is certainly one of the most iconic and distinctive. So much so, that the first series of Barbie dolls was called *Ponytail*. This hairstyle was created by Larry German, a famous stylist at Universal Studios in Hollywood. Accustomed to styling movie-stars, Larry created a practical hairdo that was also elegant and evoked a sense of youthfulness. In fact, before the 1960s, most girls and babies wore their hair in ties.

Barbie's iconic ponytail remained unchanged until the end of 1964, when her curly bangs were replaced by a side part on the *Barbie Swirl* version, a hairstyle designed by stylist Jean Ann Burger.

1960

# Solo in the Spotlight Barbie

**ICONIC ELEMENT:** MERMAID GOWN

In the first decade of the 20th century, avant-garde fashion also meant freedom. This was the case for Madeleine Vionnet, the French designer who created the mermaid dress and waged an all-out war against corsets, which were the norm for elegant clothes at the time. Vionnet introduced the practice of cutting fabric on the bias—which up to then had only been used for collars—into dressmaking. Thanks to her, dressmakers started cutting fabric diagonally at a 45-degree angle instead of following the warp of the fabric. This way, construction became more flexible, allowing patterns to be created with draping that conformed better to

## 1960

the body and avoided the discomfort of corsets. Hence the arrival of the tight-fitting dress made famous by Hollywood stars of the 1930s and '40s. Barbie paid tribute to this revolutionary style with her *Solo in the Spotlight* outfit. A black strapless dress embellished with glitter and a tulle frill was paired with a small pink chiffon scarf, black open-toe pumps, long black satin gloves, and a sparkling necklace. A silver microphone completed the look of a sophisticated singer, immediately transporting us to the refined atmosphere of New York jazz clubs.

**FUN FACT:** At the Los Angeles premiere of the film, *Barbie*, Margot Robbie wore a red-carpet look that was flawlessly inspired by this set, created by the fashion house Schiaparelli.

1960

# Enchanted Evening Barbie

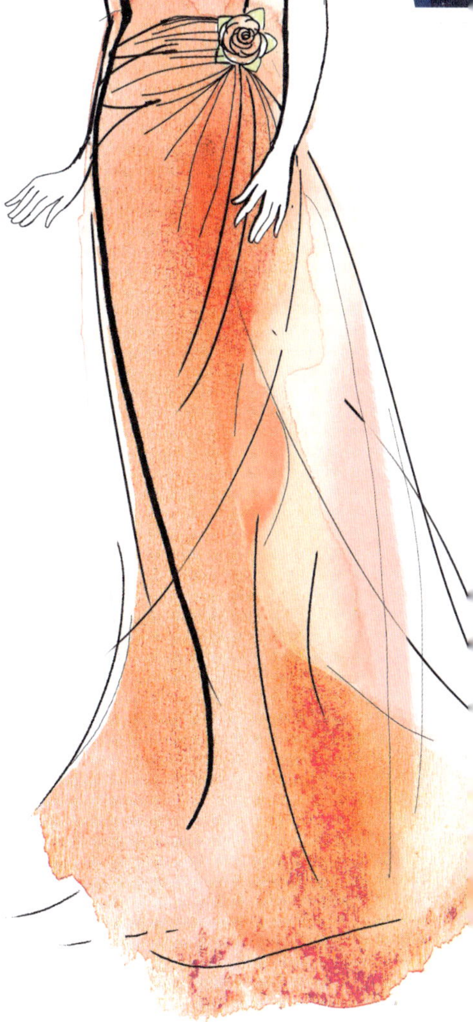

**STYLE:** GRAND SOIRÉE

Barbie played the leading role in a social life filled with big events and major galas. For these occasions, it was essential that she wear something truly captivating. Hence the arrival of her Enchanted Evening gown.

The princess archetype entered the modern era with Barbie. She was a contemporary girl who moved between work commitments, travel and lively occasions, and events that were even more spectacular than in fairy tales because they were possible. Her iconic pale pink satin gown—featuring a bodice with a

1960

fold-over hem and a long train draped on the left side—were an invitation to dream about attending an enchanting party with the poise of a princess who, in the daytime, was also a young, professional, independent, and successful woman. The accessories for this outfit were regal, too: the fabric rose that decorated the waist, the fur stole that was white, like the long gloves, along with the pearl necklace and earrings, added a special light to Barbie's look. Clearly, she was ready to enchant everyone with her matchless elegance.

1962

# Brunette Bubble Cut Barbie

**LIFESTYLE:** SOPHISTICATED ELEGANCE

**ICONIC ELEMENT:** BROWN, BOUFFANT HAIR

**INSPIRATION:** JACKIE KENNEDY AND MARILYN MONROE

It was 1962 and the women Americans admired the most were First Lady Jackie Kennedy and diva Marilyn Monroe. They had many things in common. Both were very famous women with a great sense of style, and they also shared the same hairdresser, the brilliant New York hairstylist Kenneth Battelle. Battelle created their short, soft bouffant hairstyles, which became the basis of their incomparable glamour. And while Jackie's look became the most admired one of the new decade, Barbie's style for her 1960s debut was no less aspirational. *Bubble Cut Barbie* boasted dark, short, rounded hair on her head.

## 1962

A dashing red velvet coat with a bell-shaped silhouette, a clutch fastened with a precious stone, and black pumps completed her look. But there was one more iconic element in *Bubble Cut Barbie's* look—the pillbox hat resting on her head. This style of hat was a constant presence in Jackie Kennedy's flawless appearance. From the day of the inauguration at the White House, the First Lady coordinated her suits with this understated but highly recognizable style of headwear, making it a powerful, emblematic accessory. So much so that many first ladies since Jackie Kennedy adopted it to emulate her style. For the pillbox hat was *her* hat, yet another accessory that contributed to creating the immortal image of a heroine of manners and fashion. For *Bubble Cut Barbie*, looking like Jackie was not only a matter of style but also of values and aspirations. In the society of those times, the First Lady represented the quintessentially successful woman. This example and these aspirations were what *Bubble Cut Barbie* brought into the bedrooms of American children in the 1960s.

1962

# Automobile

**IMPORTANCE:** BARBIE'S FIRST CAR

**INSPIRATION:** '60S SPORTS CAR

**ICONIC ELEMENT:** PINK CHASSIS

Mattel introduced Barbie's first car, Barbie's Austin-Healey Roadster, in 1962, three years after they launched the first doll. This elegant convertible was a style icon and perfectly in line with the sophisticated, fashionable aesthetic that had characterized Barbie's image from the moment of her debut. The lines of the car recalled the elegant lines of sports cars of the time, with luxurious details and high-quality finishing touches.

With its white vinyl seats and transparent windshield, this was a full-fledged luxury accessory for Barbie and her adventures. But it wasn't just a simple toy. Barbie's first car represented a sense of freedom and independence, as it let her travel on her own to explore anywhere she wanted. This vehicle's launch marked a turning point in Barbie's experience, introducing a new dimension that captured the imaginations of many generations.

In the United States at the time, men drove twice as many miles as women. Putting Barbie behind the wheel was a small, but powerful

1962

driving force in liberating millions of girls. Many other vehicles with widely differing designs and always with cutting-edge features followed Barbie's Austin-Healey Roadster, but they all shared the same purpose: to show that Barbie could take control of her own destiny.

1963

# Midge

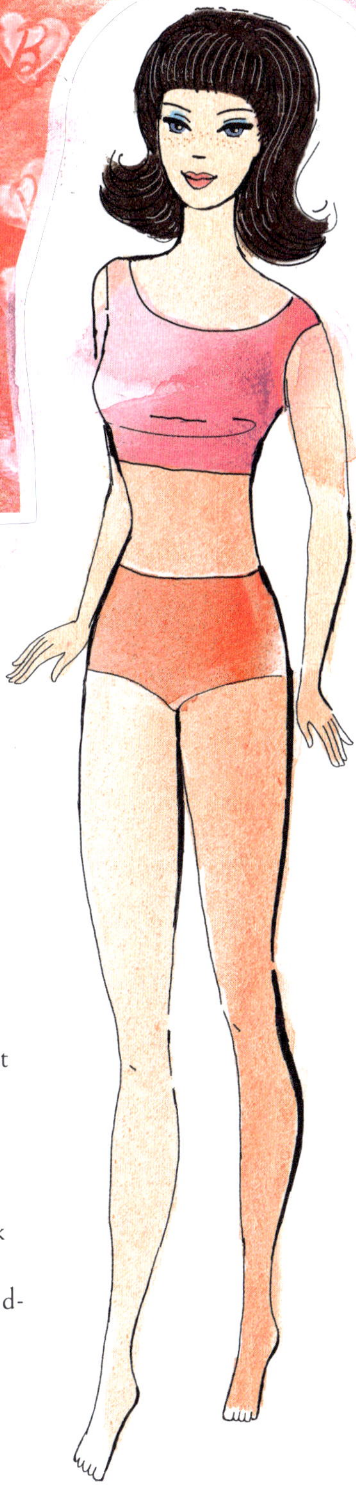

**FULL NAME:** MARGARET HADLEY SHERWOOD

**SIGNIFICANCE:** BARBIE'S FIRST FRIEND

**LIFESTYLE:** GIRL NEXT DOOR

**BOYFRIEND:** ALLAN

In 1963, Margaret "Midge" Hadley Sherwood was the first friend to join the Barbie universe. Introduced as Barbie's best friend, Midge shared Barbie's enormous wardrobe and had a boyfriend called Allan, who she built a family with.

The first version in 1963 came in three variations: the brunette with a red-and-pink bikini; the blond with a blue-and-turquoise swimsuit; and the redhead with a yellow-and-red two-piece.

## 1963

Midge had the same features as Barbie, which was why they could exchange outfits. This innovation increased children's options for play and creativity. Midge remained in production until 1966. Then in 1988, almost twenty-five years later, she returned, married to Allan, her longtime boyfriend.

1964

# Allan

**SIGNIFICANCE:** KEN'S FIRST FRIEND

**ICONIC ELEMENT:** TERRYCLOTH SHIRT

**STYLE:** BOY NEXT DOOR

**GIRLFRIEND:** MIDGE

Allan Sherwood appeared in 1964. Introduced as Ken's best friend, he was also Midge's boyfriend. In his first edition, he wore an iconic shirt with multicolored horizontal stripes and terrycloth interior, and blue swim trunks. As was the case with Barbie and Midge, Allan shared his wardrobe with Ken, which allowed children to use the two dolls' clothing interchangeably. In a sense, Allan and Midge formed a parallel couple to that of Ken and Barbie.

## 1964

While the latter led glamorous, adventurous lives, Midge and Allan had a different, family-oriented lifestyle.

# Beach wear

Barbie's first outfit was a swimsuit, a one-piece with a black-and-white chevron pattern. Lycra was relatively new in the fashion world of that time. First adopted for women's stockings due to its elasticity and durability, it then came to be used for beachwear designs, literally changing the habits of millions of women, who were used to wearing heavy, uncomfortable knit swimsuits that neither allowed freedom of movement nor dried easily.
Barbie's debut look celebrated this innovation, thus introducing her to the world as a trendsetter.
Over the years, Barbie has worn many swimsuits that followed the

fashions and habits of different eras. Just think of *Malibu Barbie* who, like a real surfer, wore a one-piece similar to a wetsuit. This look was in vogue in the 1970s among the sporty young women who surfed on the beaches of California. Barbie's first outfit was considered so iconic that for the 50th anniversary of Sports Illustrated USA, the magazine put Barbie on the cover in that 1959 swimsuit.

1964

# Black Magic Barbie

**INSPIRATION:**
AUDREY HEPBURN

In 1926, Vogue America revealed a sketch of a little black dress in crepe de chine, designed by Coco Chanel, and described it as "the dress everyone will wear." This was the start of the Little Black Dress or LBD—the one true staple, worn by everyone in the fashion world. Essential and simple, but infinitely chic thanks to its uncluttered sobriety, the Little Black Dress is still a must-have for a woman's wardrobe and continues to inspire endless variations on the theme. In addition to the style, the color of the dress was also revolutionary; thanks to Coco Chanel, for the first time in fashion history, black could be worn for any occasion.

## 1964

Vogue's prediction came true in the 1960s, thanks to Audrey Hepburn who wore a Little Black Dress in the film *Breakfast at Tiffany's*. Everyone wanted the sophisticated elegance of this article of clothing, which is like a canvas to build your own personal style on. And that's what Barbie did with the *Black Magic Ensemble*: pairing a sleek and shiny Little Black Dress, featuring a back zipper, with a tulle cape that had a bow at the collar, black gloves, gold purse, and open-toe pumps. Many people maintain that this outfit was the favorite of Ruth Handler, Barbie's creator. It was definitely chic and versatile. As Karl Lagerfeld said, "One is never overdressed or underdressed with a Little Black Dress."

1964

# Skipper

**SIGNIFICANCE:** BARBIE'S FIRST SISTER

Over the years, new characters that created a rich, complex history and expanded the possibilities for play and imagination were introduced into Barbie's world. Barbie's first and most famous sister, Skipper, appeared in 1964, increasing the size of Barbie's family. The first Skipper turned up as an eight-year-old with long hair, bangs, and a sailor-style romper suit.

Over the years, Skipper has grown and passed through multiple adolescent ages before reaching the age of 16 in 1997.

In her current version, Skipper Madison Roberts is a relaxed teenager with her feet on the ground, who likes technology

## 1964

and has accessories such as a computer, tablet, and headphones. She loves animals and babies, and her main job is babysitting.

1965

# Miss Astronaut Barbie

**SIGNIFICANCE:** THE FIRST ASTRONAUT DOLL

**INSPIRATION:** THE SPACE RACE

A new outfit for a doll, a giant leap for girls worldwide. For this Barbie model it really was fitting to paraphrase this legendary quote from the 1969 lunar landing. Four years ahead of history, Barbie flew into space. In a sense, she was the second woman to do so, after Russian cosmonaut Valentina Tereshkova in 1963. In a world dominated by men, Barbie didn't hesitate to launch herself into the space race that fired up the U.S. in the 1960s, as they competed with the Soviet Union for first place in space exploration.

Mattel beat NASA to the punch, sending Barbie into space in a silver space suit, leather boots, gloves, and buckles, and a white helmet.

## 1965

This let her small fans infinitely expand the boundaries of their imaginations and what a woman could do. Barbie also had the honor of being the first doll to go to space. In 2022, fifty-seven years after this pioneering model, Barbie really did fly into space when she took off on the DreamStar Mission to the International Space Station. Two dolls went on the mission to encourage girls from around the world to pursue careers in aerospace and, more generally, in STEM (Science, Technology, Engineering, and Mathematics) fields where women are still underrepresented.

1967

# Stripes Away Barbie

**SIGNIFICANCE:** BARBIE'S FIRST COLOR-CHANGING DRESS

In 1966, Barbie had been around for seven years. Technology during this period had made huge advances in all fields, including cosmetics. It was the era of mass production. Every day, new products were born. Some were destined to last, others were so extravagant that they quickly disappeared from the market. There were many beauty products that let you play with your own style, like changing hair color.

And this was how the most sought-after doll in the world embraced innovation.

The 1966 *Color Magic Barbie* allowed children to reversibly change Barbie's hair color. Her blond hair turned a fiery red when it came into contact with a solution sold with the doll, while the brunette Barbie's hair turned a dark red. Using another liquid solution afterwards turned the

## 1967

color back to its original shade. The same principle was also applied to *Color Magic Barbie's* outfits, among which the most iconic was definitely *Stripes Away*, a long dress with a pattern of wavy green, cherry, and melon stripes in all-out '60s optical art style. When the green stripes came into contact with the solution, they turned purple, which let children play with style and experiment with their dolls. However, the experiment didn't last. These models were only available for two years, which makes the *Color Magic Barbie* extremely rare and much-sought-after by collectors.

1967

# Twist 'n Turn Barbie

**ICONIC ELEMENT:** VINYL SWIMSUIT

**SIGNIFICANCE:** THE FIRST ARTICULATED BARBIE

**INSPIRATION:** BRITISH MOD STYLE

The twist was all the rage on dance floors and *Twist 'n Turn Barbie* became its queen. So that she could bust a move, this new doll could tilt her head and body, thanks to an articulated waist and swivel neck. In addition, the model sported a new expression, with lighter makeup, real eyelashes, and long, smooth hair. Her style reflected the cutting-edge British mod fashion of the era, inspired by models such as Jean Shrimpton and Twiggy. This was a subculture of young rebels who loved dance, music, and elegant clothing with modern shapes, all while looking towards space exploration.

## 1967

Indeed, we were in the middle of what the design world called the Space Age—the era of space—where futuristic shapes inspired by astronauts and space ships rocketed through fashion, interior design, and style in general via metallic colors and plastic materials such as vinyl. Pioneers of this trend in fashion were French designers Pierre Cardin and André Courrèges, whose creations revolutionized runways. Barbie embraced the mod style with a two-piece orange vinyl swimsuit covered by a white nylon net and long, straight hair with bangs. A true mod girl, Barbie could dance, too; her brand-new joints allowed her to assume a variety of poses. This remarkable innovation made her an icon of freedom and independence, inspiring girls to express their own individuality and embrace their uniqueness.

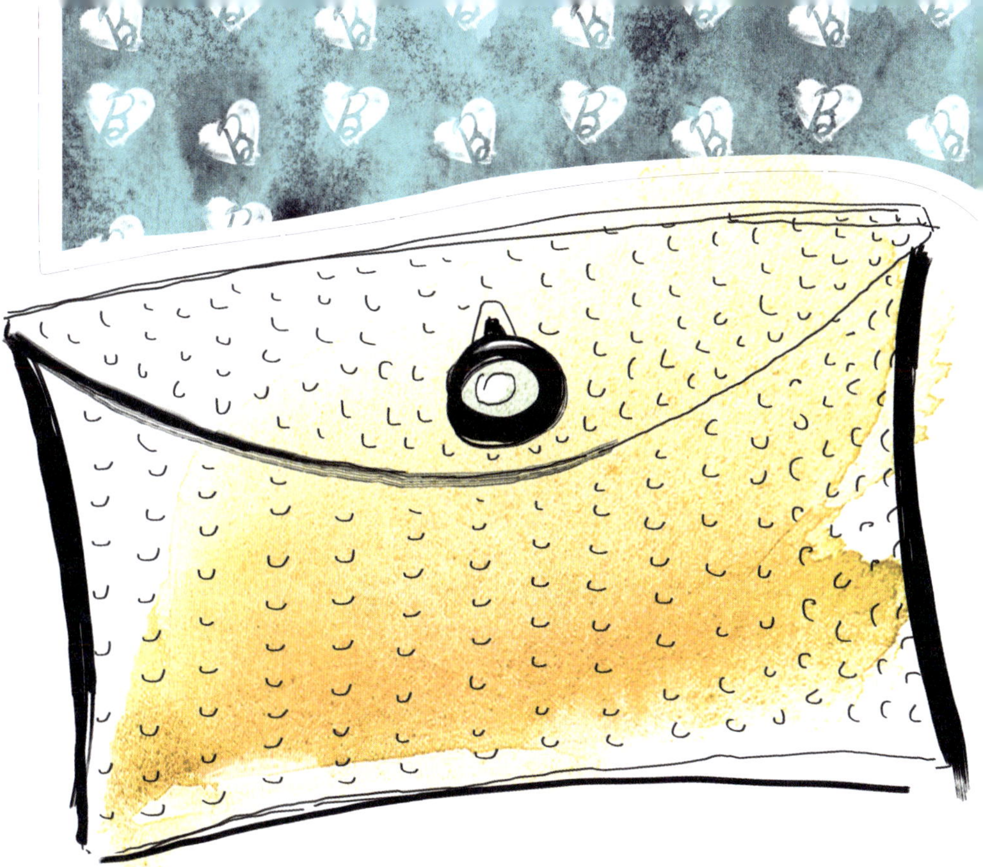

# Bags

**ICONIC ELEMENT:** THE CLUTCH FROM THE 1962 RED FLARE OUTFIT

**SIGNIFICANCE:** A BAG FOR EVERY OCCASION

"If there's one thing that has resisted mechanical improvement since medieval times, it's a woman's purse," wrote Isaac Asimov in *The Caves of Steel*. While the science-fiction master was probably not an expert in glamour, his statement is certainly true. Starting with her 1962 *Red Flare* outfit, Barbie's accessories often included a purse. Evening bags, clutches, shoulder bags, briefcases, doctors' cases, and roller bags: Barbie has had many bags in her wardrobe. Time and time again, Barbie's designers conveyed the moods and society she inhabited via this attention to detail.

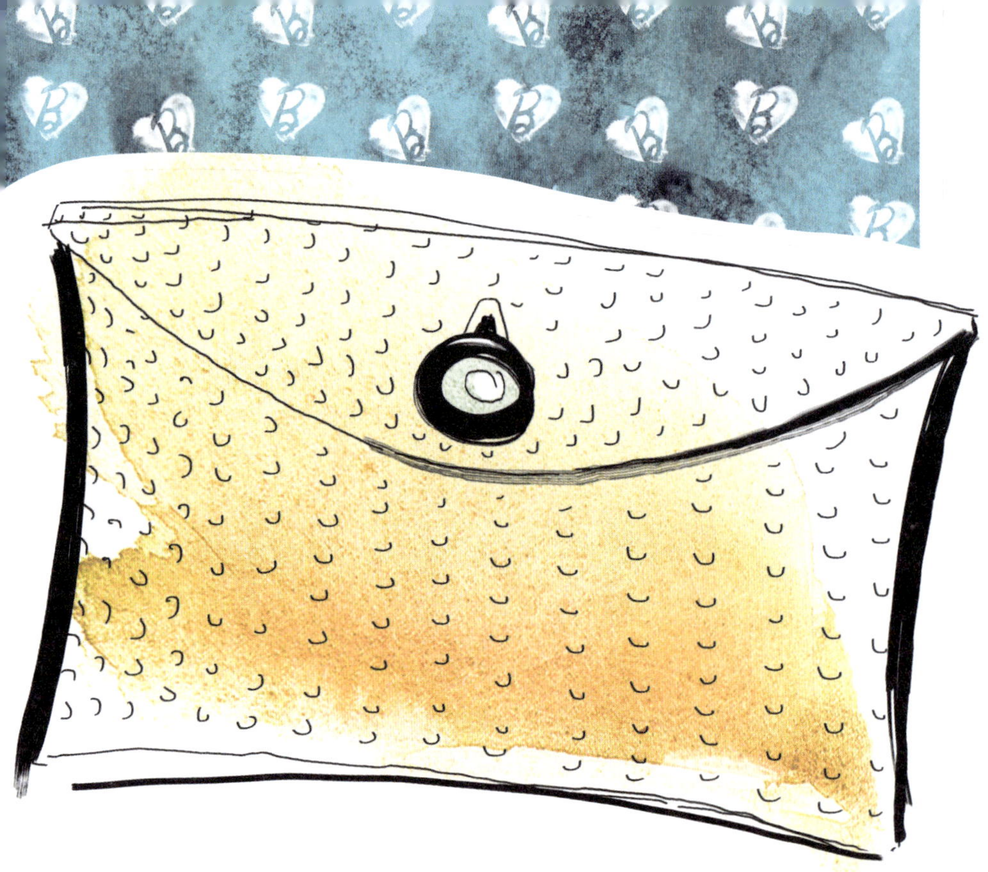

Indeed, no look would be complete without the accessories that match the theme and atmosphere. Whether it's for a gala or a trip to the beach, there's always a purse to suit the occasion.

**FUN FACT:** From earrings to shoes, everything is designed by hand and then sculpted in wax to create 3D models.

## 1968

# Jump Into Lace Barbie

**ICONIC ELEMENT:** PALAZZO PAJAMAS

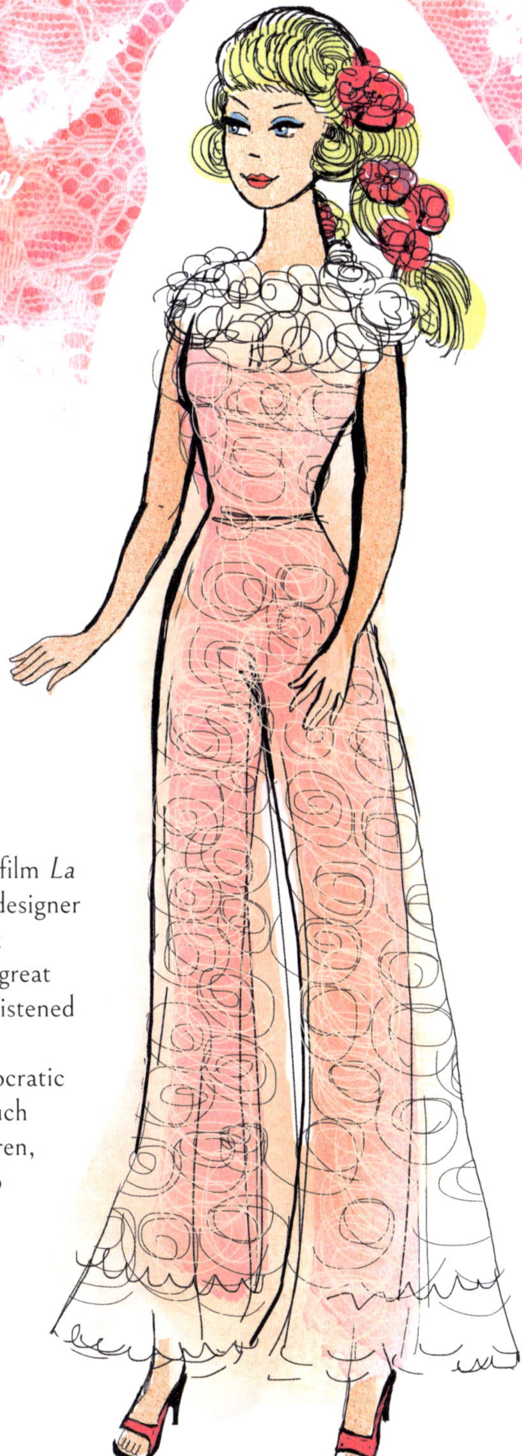

It was 1960, the year of the classic film *La Dolce Vita*. In Florence, princess-designer Irene Galitzine introduced roomy silk jumpsuits in gaudy colors, which the great fashion journalist Diana Vreeland christened "palazzo pajamas."

The garment first won over the aristocratic women of Rome, then movie stars such as Claudia Cardinale and Sophia Loren, and finally even Jackie Kennedy, who brought it back to the U.S., making it an instant must-have item for the leading ladies of the jet set. The palazzo pajama was a major transformation, a reinterpretation of traditional eveningwear that turned comfort

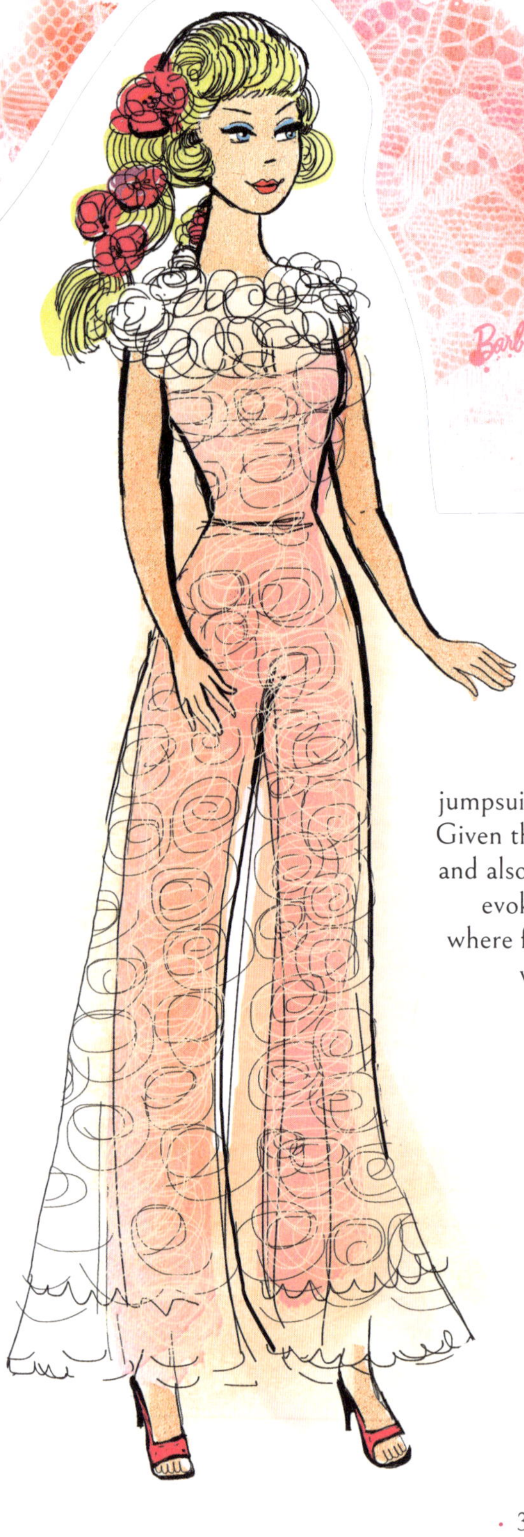

## 1968

and a lack of restriction into a style manifesto. The cut of the *Jump Into Lace* jumpsuit recalled the lines of palazzo pajamas, reinterpreted with a Barbie twist: a pink taffeta jumpsuit with an intricate white lace overlay. Given that "jump" is both short for jumpsuit and also means "to leap," the name naturally evoked Barbie's dynamic, stylish life, one where fashion becomes a way to express her values of freedom and empowerment.

# DreamHouse

**SIGNIFICANCE:**
BARBIE'S FIRST HOUSE

Named the DreamHouse, Barbie's first house was launched in 1962 and cost $4 (USD) to buy. The DreamHouse was revolutionary, as in those days, a woman's right to buy a home on her own was not yet protected by the Fair Housing Act of 1968. Barbie not only owned this fabulous house, but clearly, she also lived independently.

Despite its simple cardboard construction, the DreamHouse was fully equipped with great care in true '60s style.

To understand the level of detail, you just had to see the miniature clothes hangers in the closet and the tiny books on the shelves.

Over time, the details and materials in the DreamHouse evolved to

reflect innovations and new lifestyles. In the '60s, the newest feature was a TV; in the '70s, it was an elevator, and in the '90s, the elevator was electrified. More recently, the DreamHouse has included a pool with a slide, a play area for puppies, and a party room. The DreamHouse multiplied the options for creating and playing with Barbie's stories. It was also an opportunity to dream of an independent adult life. Having an environment that reflected your own tastes and interests was essential for building a sense of self, as much for girls as for the adults they would become.

1971

# Malibu Ken

**SIGNIFICANCE:** THE FIRST KEN WITH BENDABLE LEGS

**STYLE:** SURFER

From Barbie's debut in 1959, Mattel worked to build a three-dimensional world around her, from family members to pets, friends, and her boyfriend. Ken first appeared in 1961. The two met on the set of their first commercial, and they would be inseparable from then until their breakup in 2004.

Ken was two years and two days younger than Barbie, and his name was a tribute from Barbie's creator to her son. In his first version, Ken wore red swim trunks, sandals, and a yellow towel, and he had a wardrobe of seven outfits.

Much like his girlfriend, Ken has explored a wide variety of styles and professions throughout his history.

## 1971

Hence, Malibu Ken arrived soon after Malibu Barbie—tanned and with bendable legs that let him surf the waves and enjoy beach life. With his red shorts and blue beach towel, Malibu Ken paid homage to the first Ken, who entered imaginations so fully that he was on the market until 1978.

## 1971

# Malibu Barbie

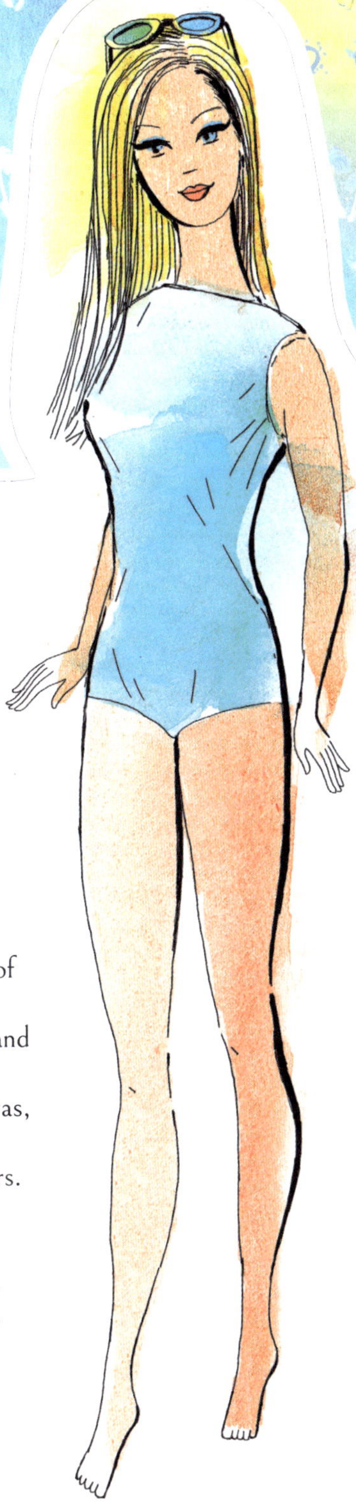

**ACCESSORIES:** SURFER'S SWIMSUIT AND BEACH TOWEL

**SIGNIFICANCE:** THE FIRST SMILING BARBIE

**INSPIRATION:** SURF CULTURE

From the beginning, Barbie specialized in exciting seaside vacations. In the 1970s, one of the most popular destinations for young people in America (and elsewhere!) was certainly Malibu, and Barbie was its ultimate star.

This magical seaside town outside Los Angeles was, in those days, a paradise for surfers searching for waves and a glamorous refuge for Hollywood stars. As early as the 1920s, Malibu was a favorite destination for surfing pioneers, and by the late 1950s, it had become the cradle of surf culture, a symbol of the California dream made of sun, sea, and carefree happiness.

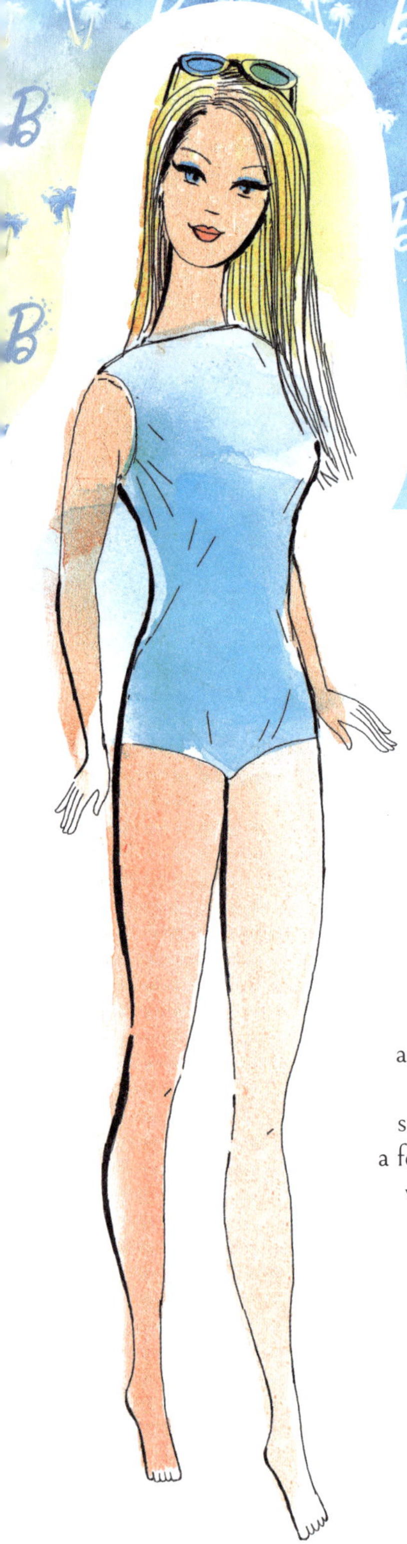

## 1971

But it wasn't until the early 1970s that surfing began to magnetically attract young people, becoming an authentic lifestyle made of physical activity, music, and style, and strong values. In fact, the young people who comprised the Malibu surfing community weren't just strong, well-adjusted beach bums who could ride the waves. They were also passionate environmentalists and became real counterculture icons of the time. Barbie celebrated Malibu, its culture, and its lifestyle with some important changes. A new pearly white smile appeared on her tanned face and for the first time, her gaze, as blue as the sea, faced forward. With her long hair and dazzling smile, Malibu Barbie was not merely a surfer, but a fearless, liberated young woman, like many young women of the time who were surfing the wave of feminism and female empowerment.

# Dream Camper

**IMPORTANCE:** BARBIE'S FIRST CAMPER VAN

It was the era of road trips and women's lib: Barbie combined these two trends with a brand-new, shiny and vibrant camper to explore the world in.

Barbie's first Dream Camper was a true home on wheels. It came fully equipped and included a kitchenette, a picnic set with seats and a little table, pop-out tent, sleeping bags, and a roof rack.

Over the years, the Dream Camper became one of Barbie's constant accessories. In fact, in the decades that followed, several different editions were produced—packed with accessories that kept up with the times—as well as themed versions, such as the beach camper, the tour bus, and the party bus.

From the moment it was launched, the Dream Camper became a much

sought-after accessory for Barbie fans worldwide. But this very first model told us something more: it was a tangible sign of the growth in Barbie's personality, aspirations, and lifestyle, which grew ever more adventurous, independent, and liberated. As a result, the play-style with this new accessory could also be more active, inviting children to enjoy adventure and the great outdoors, and shared experiences—inspiring endless travel stories.

**FUN FACT:** In Malibu, California, there was a real-life Dream Camper, inspired by the toy, where guests could actually stay.

# 1971

## Live Action Barbie

**STYLE:** FLOWER CHILD

**SIGNIFICANCE:** THE FIRST DANCING BARBIE

**INSPIRATION:** THE LEGENDARY 1969 WOODSTOCK FESTIVAL

The 1970s were a time of great cultural change. Consequently, Barbie came in many different versions. One of these was *Live Action Barbie*, a doll designed to move and dance as never before, thanks also to the Touch ’n Go stand, which let her move to the rhythm of the music. Two years after the large musical gathering at Woodstock, which marked not just the generation that attended it but also those to come, Barbie sported a true

## 1971

flower child look, with flared pants and brightly patterned sleeves. With this bold outfit, her long hair, and big, sparkling eyes, *Live Action Barbie* reflected the allure and excitement of 1970s fashion and culture, conveying the sense of freedom and joy of those years. As with the other models from this decade, and in keeping with the rise of feminism, *Live Action Barbie* depicted an independent, bold, self-confident woman who strove to realize her own dreams and pursue her own success in an ever-changing world.

1974

# St. Moritz Barbie

**INSPIRATION:** *APRÈS SKI*

In the 1970s, spending a winter vacation in St. Moritz was the ultimate in chic. From European aristocrats to music and movie stars, the international jet set met at this famous Swiss resort for luxury vacations filled with sports, relaxation, and nightlife. During this period, the snow-clad ski slopes were filled with colorful ski suits, the trendiest of which were designed by Emilio Pucci. In the town center's well-known streets and salons, socialites wore iconic après-ski outfits that were simultaneously comfortable and dazzling.

## 1974

Barbie stepped into the St. Moritz holiday scene, wearing a pink ribbed jersey jumpsuit, with a turtleneck, matching cap, gold belt, boots with pink heels, a white sleeveless coat and matching purse. The result? Pure sophistication.

**1977**

# Superstar Barbie

**ICONIC ELEMENT:** FEATHER BOA

**STYLE:** DISCO DIVA

**INSPIRATION:** FARRAH FAWCETT

The late 1970s marked the era of disco. In New York, it was the heyday of Studio 54, the most famous nightclub of all time. In the movies, John Travolta in his white suit got everyone dancing with *Saturday Night Fever*. And on dance floors around the world, people went crazy for the sophisticated, exciting sounds of the new disco music. It was the time of glitzy parties, wild fun, and maximalist outfits. Once again, Barbie dazzled the world—with *Superstar Barbie*, a new look influenced by the most elegant evening styles

## 1977

and a new facial expression inspired by Farrah Fawcett, the blond lead in the hit TV series *Charlie's Angels*. With Superstar, the image of Barbie was crystallized in the collective imagination, an image that will probably remain her most iconic one across the years—a stunning long pink dress, blond hair, twinkling blue eyes, and sparkling jewelry. Ready to dance the night away, *Superstar Barbie* embodied the bold, exuberant spirit of '70s fashion, which moved away from the styles and cultural upheavals of the 1960s and early '70s and anticipated the trends of the '80s. The link between *Superstar Barbie* and this historical period went beyond fashion and spilled over into pop culture: the aspiration for fame and success that permeated late '70s society was embodied in her glamorous image, and fully aligned with the myth of the American Dream.

## 1980

# Black Barbie

**SIGNIFICANCE:** THE FIRST BLACK BARBIE

**INSPIRATION:** DONNA SUMMER AND GLORIA GAYNOR

**STYLE:** DISCO MUSIC

Barbie was a reflection of contemporary culture. From the moment she was launched, she has evolved in step with fashion, trends, and society. At the peak of the civil rights movement that ended racial segregation in the U.S., Francie (in 1967) and Christie (in 1968) made their debut as Barbie's first Black friends, reflecting significant societal changes. Barbie's creators had realized she could convey specific values to children and consequently began working to broaden the diversity of the dolls, with the goal of giving all children a chance to identify themselves with the brand while avoiding stereotyped or prejudiced images.

*Black Barbie* arrived in 1980, at the height of

## 1980

the disco era. Inspired by the style of the hottest Black singers, such as Donna Summer and Gloria Gaynor, *Black Barbie* wore a red dress with a wrap skirt and a deep slit—perfect for dancing—paired with a gold necklace and dangling pendant earrings. *Black Barbie* was an important step in Barbie's history, working towards increasingly broader representation, which today includes thirty-five different skin tones, ninety-seven hairstyles, and nine body types, to better reflect the world's diversity and provide children with an ever-increasing number of role models to relate to as they grow.

## 1981

# Western Barbie

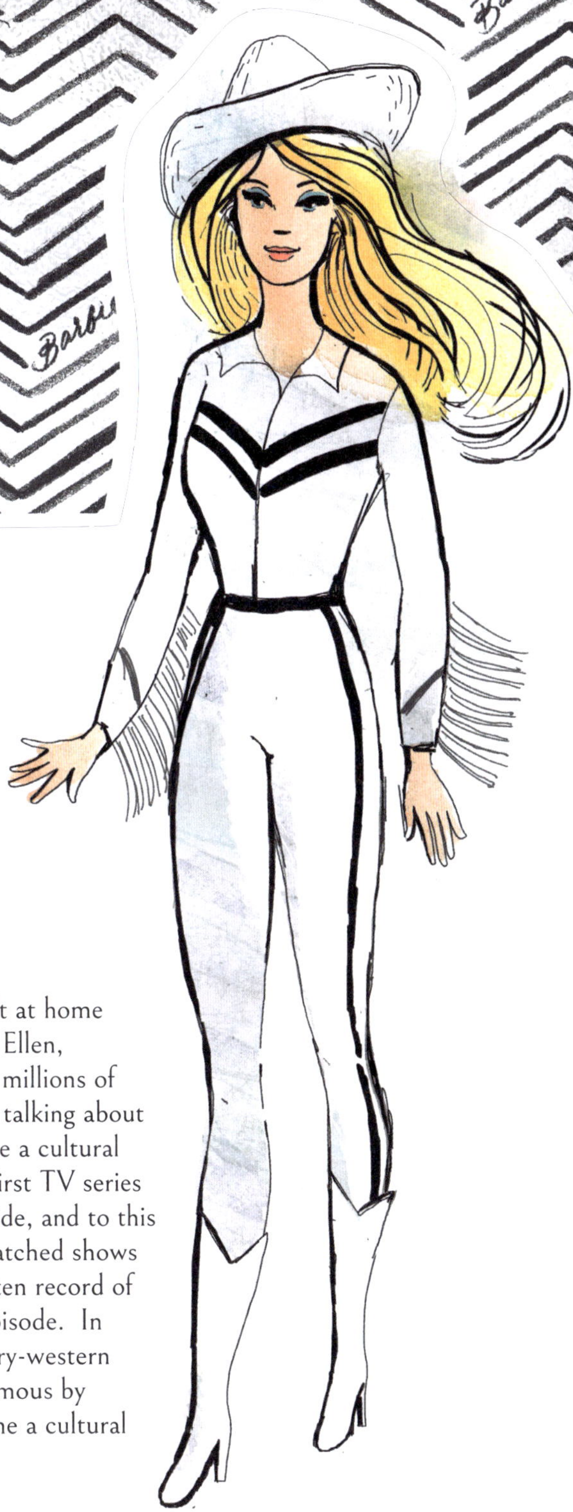

**STYLE:** TEXAN

**ACCESSORIES:** BARBIE HORSE, "DALLAS"

**INNOVATIONS:** WINKING EYES AND BUSY HANDS

By the late 1970s, everyone felt at home in Texas: the fortunes of Sue Ellen, J.R., and their oil-rich family kept millions of viewers glued to their TVs. We're talking about *Dallas*, the soap opera that became a cultural phenomenon. It was, in fact, the first TV series in history to be broadcast worldwide, and to this day, it remains one of the most-watched shows of all time, still holding the unbeaten record of 360 million viewers for a single episode. In 1981, Barbie paid tribute to country-western living and the Texan style made famous by *Dallas*—which by then had become a cultural

## 1980

touchstone—by wearing the perfect Western outfit: a white jumpsuit with black and silver details, cowboy boots, and the obligatory wide-brimmed white cowboy hat. The outfit came with a detachable Western skirt so that Barbie was always ready for both horseback riding and more festive occasions.

In terms of design, this model featured two major innovations. For the first time, Barbie could wink, thanks to a button on her back. In addition, her hands could move, something that had first appeared many years earlier and that let her grasp objects. With this essential detail, she could hold her hat and, most importantly, the reins of her horse—named Dallas, of course.

## 1982

# Fashion Jeans Barbie

**ICONIC ELEMENT:**
BARBIE'S FIRST JEANS

Canvas from Genoa and denim from Nîmes were heavy cotton fabrics that dockworkers in these two Mediterranean cities wore because they were comfortable and sturdy. Brought to the U.S. by gold prospectors in the middle of the 19th century, jeans became the quintessential work garment for dockworkers, cowboys, carpenters, and farmers. In the years after World War II, jeans started to become a fashion garment. Worn by James Dean, Elvis Presley, Brigitte Bardot, and Marilyn Monroe, jeans turned into a symbol of youthful rebellion and rock and roll. Thanks to this explosion, in a few years, jeans became an iconic unisex article of clothing. Barbie made her first appearance in jeans in the 1980s.

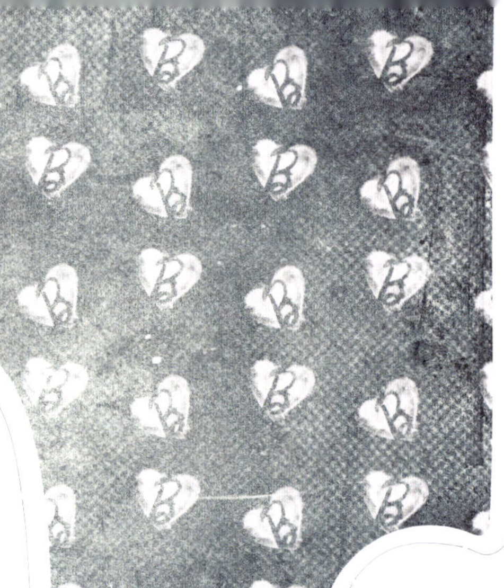

## 1982

Her face was the same as *Superstar Barbie*, but with extra-long, full, wavy hair. Barbie wore jeans personalized with her name on the back pocket and a soft pink sweater. It was the first time that Barbie wore her own logo. This would happen many more times in the following decades, a visual sign that Barbie had truly reached the status of being an icon —and not just a stylish doll.

# Cowboy boots and hat

**STYLE:** TEXAN

**INSPIRATION:** THE LOOKS OF THE CHARACTERS FROM THE TV SERIES *DALLAS*

**ICONIC ELEMENT:** PINK, FOR BOTH

From the Duke of Wellington to Elvis Presley, from Dolly Parton to Miley Cyrus, the cowboy-boot trend has endured for almost three centuries.

Before becoming a fashion accessory, cowboy boots fit the different needs that they were worn for, combining form and function: they're stiff, made of tough leather that protects from snake bites, and have curved soles that end in an upward-pointing tip, to make mounting a horse easier. Another iconic piece of traditional Texan attire is the hat: a classic wide-brimmed head covering that is an essential part of the cowboy look—not just in the popular imagination, but in real life too.

The cowboy hat has been widely popular since its creation in the 19th century, thanks to its practical design: its wide brim protects wearers from both sun and rain. Cowboy boots and cowboy hats have been part of Barbie's wardrobe since 1980. Naturally, she gave them her signature stylish twist—reimagining them in pink, adding glitter and jewelled details and helping to cement the iconic status of these two timeless American accessories.

**FUN FACT:** The creases in a cowboy hat make it more comfortable, but they also personalize it, becoming a distinctive feature by which someone can be recognized, even at a distance.

1983

# Crystal Barbie

**CLAIM:** "SHE SHINES WITH GLAMOUR FROM HEAD TO TOE!"

**ICONIC ELEMENT:** A NECKLACE JUST LIKE BARBIE'S FOR CHILDREN TO WEAR

Chiffon, glitter, tulle, and maximalist volume—in other words, the 1980s! It was a time of excess and uncompromising style, and *Crystal Barbie* fully embodied it: a triumph of light and shimmer in pure '80s style.

## 1983

Full and iridescent, her grand soirée outfit featured a ruffle at the bottom and dramatic tulle shoulder straps. Her shoes were silver, as was her jewelry, which was embellished with luminous white pearls. It was the perfect outfit for enchanting evenings, memorable ceremonies, elegant balls, and special occasions. And this doll came with a special feature: inside each box was a child-sized crystal necklace!

1985

# Day-to-Night Barbie

**ICONIC ELEMENT:**
TWO-IN-ONE FASHION

The 1980s were a decade of excess. Everything was bigger and bolder, including volumes, saturated color, lots of jewelry, and carefully styled hair. People dressed for success at work and flaunted designer clothes and accessories. Power dressing, a key '80s trend, led to tailored jackets with shoulder pads that created an angular, often-exaggerated look. The women's power suit, made popular by designers such as Giorgio Armani and Valentino, was often complemented by a matching handbag and shoes. *Day-to-Night Barbie* was a busy career woman,

## 1985

ready to go out to a thrilling social event after a quick outfit change. Her outfit began with a bright pink suit, complete with a wide-brimmed hat and briefcase. Because it was reversible, the suit turned into a pink chiffon skirt and metallic top, perfect for an exciting evening. *Day-to-Night Barbie's* quick-change ability was reminiscent of her 1959 commuter set. Both outfits let the icon be the star of her day, from morning to night.

1986

# Barbie & the Rockers

**SIGNIFICANCE:** BARBIE'S FIRST ROCK BAND

**STYLE:** GLAM ROCK

Iconic albums, immortal hits, and stunning looks: these were the '80s. In this era, rock fused with pop. Songs became catchier, fully capturing the new musical taste of a generation that wanted to have fun. The guitar remained front and center, but there was also room for new sounds, experiments, and the use of synthesizers, all typified by Depeche Mode, Spandau Ballet, Duran Duran, and Guns N' Roses. Girls and boys around the world spent hours every day glued to their walkmans via headphones and emulated their music idols' hairstyles and clothing.
Hot on the heels of this trend, Mattel introduced the successful *Barbie & the Rockers* series, a genuine '80s glam band. Neon colors, shoulder

## 1985

pads, and big hair paid tribute to the styles of the day. Barbie, Diva, Dana, and Dee Dee wore bright neon-colored leggings, belts, oversized blazers, and puffy bows in their big hair. Even the makeup reflected the trends of the time with bright eyeshadows and lipstick. Derek, the boy in the group, wore classic '80s pants—wide at the hips and narrow at the bottom—paired with a lamé sash, a flashy tailcoat jacket and big hair. A neon-colored shirt and leg warmers completed his look.

# Scooter

**ICONIC ELEMENT:**
PERSONALIZED STICKER

**SIGNIFICANCE:** BARBIE'S FIRST SCOOTER

Since the iconic movie *Roman Holiday*, getting around on a scooter has been synonymous with freedom and glamour. Originally an economic vehicle in the post-World War II period, the scooter became a symbol of Italian design and a specific way of living everyday life—with lightheartedness, flexibility, and a touch of romanticism.

Riding a scooter meant seeing the world with a more poetic point of view, feeling the wind in your face, enjoying the city from a different angle, and feeling it flow around you.

In 1978, Barbie embraced the vitality of this means of transport with her first scooter. The StarCycle was pink and white, with a front basket personalized by a sticker ... a two-wheeled summary of Barbie's style.

Over the years, the scooter models have been updated with newer colors and designs, but the dynamic attitude characterizing this accessory has remained unchanged: just put Barbie on the seat of her scooter and she will speed toward a world of imagination and fun, where the possibilities are infinite.

# Jewelry

**ICONIC ELEMENT:**
PLAYFUL CHARM

**SIGNIFICANCE:** ACCESSORIES FOUND ON VIRTUALLY EVERY BARBIE

Starting in 1959 with the very first model that sported iconic round earrings, Barbie's looks have been accessorized with real miniature pieces of jewelry, which enhance her sparkle and style, and contribute to her timeless elegance. Pearls, diamonds, gemstones, gold, and silver: Barbie's jewelry has explored the whole spectrum of gems and precious metals, including both iconic cuts from the world of fine jewelry and also simple, everyday pieces to complete her look. Just about every Barbie model has worn jewelry, be it minimalist or maximalist, showing the care and attention to detail that goes into planning every doll. They also add an additional layer of play: swapping jewelry between dolls, putting it on and taking it off, offers a fun way to play with fashion. Interestingly, while the jewelry Barbie wore originally was based on real world examples, the emergence of the Barbiecore trend—an aesthetic inspired by Barbie—sparked the reverse process. Fine jewelry and costume jewelry makers

drew their inspiration from the world of Barbie, creating pieces aligned with her style, one of self-confident, playful charm.

**FUN FACT:** Making the small components that accessorize Barbie's outfits—from jewelry to zippers and buttons—is no mean feat. It requires highly skilled workmanship, for which Mattel relies on a Japanese company, YKK, which specializes in producing small-scale accessories.

## 1987

# Surf

**STYLE:**
URBAN

**ICONIC ELEMENTS:**
VIBRANT PATTERNS AND ACCESSORIES

**INSPIRATION:** LATE '80S FASHION

Unlike previous beach-themed dolls, the ones in the *California Dream* line didn't just sport swimsuits; they featured trendy outfits emblematic of Californian youth—active, lively, fun-loving young people who enjoyed the company of others. With her sleeveless shirt, ruffled circle skirt, hi-tops, leg warmers, visor and sunglasses, Barbie summed up late '80s fashion, which consisted of geometric patterns and colorful accessories—most memorably, plastic palm-tree shaped earrings and a vinyl, disc-shaped bag.

Ready to walk along the loveliest California beaches to meet her friends Ken, Teresa, and Christie, *California Dream Barbie* brought her hobbies with her, too, shown by her choice of accessories—a camera and a Frisbee.

## 1987

The vivid Surf Shop and unique hot dog stand completed the scene in pure '80s California style, with the latter made in the shape of the typical frankfurter in a bun. Together, they rounded out this super-cool lifestyle made up of sports, relaxation, and friendship.

# 1988

## Teresa

**SIGNIFICANCE:** BARBIE'S FIRST LATINA FRIEND

In 1988, Teresa Rivera made her first appearance on the flashy, iconic *California Dream* set. From that moment on, she has been at Barbie's side in the many versions that have continued to today, including *Rollerblade Teresa*, *Happenin' Hair Teresa*, and *Camp Teresa*. She has also starred in a number of special editions celebrating her Latina culture, including *Quinceañera Teresa*, which honored the Latin American tradition of celebrating a girl's transition into a young woman on her fifteenth birthday. For that event,

## 1988

Teresa wore a fairy-tale dress in pink chiffon with a lace bodice, pearl necklace, and a bouquet made of lace. Like Christie, Teresa illustrated a way to celebrate the beauty of differences and to provide as many children as possible a chance to play and imagine their future by identifying themselves in the two dolls.

## 1988

# Christie

**SIGNIFICANCE:** BARBIE'S FRIEND

**ICONIC ELEMENT:** BRIGHT AND BOLD LOOK

Ever since her launch, Barbie has evolved in step with fashion, trends, and culture. In the late '60s, amidst the struggles and achievements in civil rights, Mattel began planning new dolls to accompany the popular Barbie line. These dolls marked the start of broader representation, expanding the image of success, independence, and style that had long been associated with Barbie. The first Mattel doll with a darker skin tone was Francie, a French friend of Barbie created in 1967, followed by Christie, the following year. Elegant and independent, Christie always chose bright, happy colors, unlike her boyfriend, who dressed in high style. In the '70s, she updated her look, with long hair and highlights.

## 1988

Over the years, Mattel has introduced Christie's family: her sisters Nicole (Nikki), Janet, and Deirdre, fiancé Steven, and cousins Grace and Shawnee.

# 1991

# Totally Hair Barbie

**SIGNIFICANCE:** THE BESTSELLING BARBIE IN HISTORY

**ICONIC ELEMENT:** EXTRA-LONG HAIR

In addition to inventing endless scenarios for play and projecting their hopes and dreams for the future, many children never seem to tire of playing with Barbie's hair. This discovery, which emerged from a market study, was the basis for the best-selling Barbie doll in history. *Totally Hair Barbie* celebrated the showy hairstyles of the early '90s, offering children the option of creating different hairdos, thanks to her extra-long mane (a good 11.5 inches!). The box also included a comb, several hair accessories, a tube of gel, and a booklet with many examples of hairstyles

## 1991

for inspiration. In the '70s, Mattel had already realized that children loved playing with Barbie's hair, which is why the synthetic fibers were improved again and again to make them sturdier. But this model marked the arrival of a new level of interactivity and personalization. Children could style the hair, and it was precisely this option for creativity that made *Totally Hair Barbie* a style icon, one whose success is still unrivaled today.

# Shoes

**NUMBERS:** ONE BILLION MODELS

**ICONIC ELEMENT:** PINK PUMP

**SIGNIFICANCE:** INSPIRED MODERN FASHION

How many models of shoes has Barbie worn since her 1959 debut? Anyone attempting this daunting calculation has estimated around a billion. Every outfit is always finished with a pair of shoes perfectly matched in style and color.

As with her clothing, Barbie's footwear has evolved with fashion trends. From high-heeled '50s mules to boots, sandals, ballet flats, and sneakers, Barbie has strolled through the history of fashion at a fast clip ... without ever tiring. Nevertheless, when discussing Barbie and shoes, one model overall has left a lasting impression on popular imaginations. Obviously, we're talking about pink pumps.

These pointy-toe shoes with thin heels represent Barbie's quintessential style: elegant, playful, and totally matching her signature color palette.

Over time, pink pumps have become so iconic that even great designers such as Manolo Blahnik and Christian Louboutin have reimagined them for grown-up Barbie fans.

1995

# Hot Skating Barbie

**ICONIC ELEMENT:**
INLINE SKATES

The roller-skating trend of the '80s saw an upgrade in the '90s with the introduction of inline skates, which had a single row of wheels instead of the more comfortable two-by-two setup. Keeping your balance became much harder, while tricks and style reached a whole new level. A true global craze was unleashed. Kids and teens everywhere embraced the colorful skates, using them not just for fun and freestyle tricks, but also as a new way to get around. The 1990s skater look was form-fitting and flashy: tight shorts, T-shirts

## 1995

and short tank tops, leggings, jumpsuits, and above all, the obligatory protective gear. Barbie raced into this trend with *Skater Barbie*, wearing a tight, multicolored jumpsuit, skates, knee pads, and elbow pads in pink and neon yellow. Her long, straight hair paid homage to the style of the time, as did the pattern on the jumpsuit. She's virtually a time capsule: just looking at this image takes you back to those fun, carefree days. And it makes you want to zoom along on your own roller adventure!

# Dream Wardrobe

**NUMBERS:** 120 MODELS PER YEAR

**ICONIC ELEMENT:** SEPARATELY PURCHASED OUTFITS

**SIGNIFICANCE:** A JOURNEY THROUGH THE HISTORY OF FASHION FROM THE '50S TO TODAY

Barbie's wardrobe has definitely stayed well-stocked: more than 120 new outfits are created for her every year. From the very beginning in 1959, it was clear that Barbie was not just any doll: she closely followed fashion and often created it. In her more than sixty-year history, Barbie has embraced most of the aesthetic trends and styles of the 20th century. From the '50s looks of sophisticated elegance to the new fashions of the '60s, passing through the rebellious '70s and the excesses of the '80s and '90s, she constantly changed her looks, continuing today to surprise and reflect the spirit of the times.
Producing Barbie's clothes mirrors the same creative processes used by the world's most prestigious fashion houses. Barbie's fashion designers create sketches, then build prototypes using muslin fabric and rubber mannequins.

After various tests, the process results in a prototype of the final version of the outfit, which requires great accuracy. Perhaps more than anything else, the feature that made Barbie into a fashion icon has been the ability to buy these outfits separately. Even if you only owned a single doll, you could endlessly change it, thanks to the many looks available. This possibility has given children the freedom to create their own outfits and looks, making them the stylists for their own dolls and, in turn, giving them ideas for the clothes they would wear one day.

2010

# Barbie Basics Dolls

**ICONIC ELEMENT:** TWELVE VARIATIONS ON THE LITTLE BLACK DRESS

The *Collectors Editions* celebrated the strong connection between Barbie and fashion in a specific way, through special editions intended for Barbie's adult fans. A standout example was the *Barbie Basics Dolls* line, launched in 2010 and designed by Bill Greening. Twelve carefully detailed and refined dolls, each dressed in the most essential, elegant, and timeless article of clothing in a woman's wardrobe: the Little Black Dress.

Each of the twelve dolls came with something unique. All had different hairstyles, features, and skin tones and wore a luxurious variation on the theme of the Little Black Dress.

## 2010

The collection showcased little black dresses in different lengths, with and without sleeves, featuring different draping, with V-neck, sweetheart, boat, and butterfly necklines. It was a triumph of sophistication and elegance. The makeup was reminiscent of that on the first model from 1959, the soft Silkstone plastic made it look like porcelain, and the hair was made with high-quality fiber. A tribute to the *Black Magic Ensemble* from 1964, which celebrated the sophisticated elegance of the Little Black Dress, this line was also decidedly contemporary.

# Pets

**NUMBERS:** OVER 50

**SIGNIFICANCE:** TEACHING RESPECT FOR ANIMALS

In Barbie's universe, animals are respected, petted, and treated with love like real friends. Barbie—along with her family members and close friends—has shared her life with a variety of animals, who joined her adventures and helped even the smallest children nurture a sense of love and respect for animals through play.

There have been over 50 animals in Barbie's history. Among them, she has had six horses, one Arabian stallion, three ponies, an Afghan hound, a poodle, a parrot, three puppies, and two cats. In addition, among Barbie's more than 250 careers is that of a veterinarian, which first appeared in 1996 and has since been reprised in several updated editions.

The presence of so many animals illustrates the special attention given to the subject of our relationship with nature and caring. Living with an animal means being able to count on a friendship of immeasurable value, and also nurtures a sense of responsibility and respect for others. This is a very important message for all children. Through play, they learn values that will help make the world a better place.

## 2016

# Barbie Fashionistas

**SIGNIFICANCE:** CHAMPIONS OF DIVERSITY

Barbie reflects contemporary culture not only in fashion, but also in social awareness and sensibilities. For this reason, the Barbie Fashionistas line was launched in 2016, the most significant, revolutionary change in Barbie's recent history. That year marked the debut of dolls with three new body types (tall, petite, and curvy), seven skin tones, 22 eye shades, and 24 different hairstyles, from naturally curly to shaved. The feet were adjustable so that they could wear both heels and flat shoes like sneakers, sandals, and ballet flats. There were also fifteen new versions of Ken, with three different body types, seven skin tones, nine face shapes, eight hair colors and nine hairstyles.

## 2016

*Barbie Fashionistas* were champions of diversity and inclusion as never before: a sign of the awareness of changing times and a new possibility for children—and former children—around the world to see themselves reflected and feel represented by a true style icon.

2018

# Frida Kahlo Barbie

**SIGNIFICANCE:** ONE OF THE INSPIRING WOMEN MATTEL CHOSE AS A ROLE MODEL FOR GIRLS OF TODAY

For International Women's Day in 2018, Barbie launched the *Inspiring Women* line, a series of dolls dedicated to celebrating the strength and passion of female figures who redefined the role of women in the world. The Mexican painter Frida Kahlo stands out among these women. Her life and works are examples of determination, courage, and unlimited creativity.

## 2018

Frida is a positive model of strength for women around the world. She overcame immense hardship and physical pain caused by disease and an accident she suffered at a young age. Throughout everything, she never lost her desire to be an artist. With her palette of vibrant colors and iconic mix of reality and fantasy, she addressed important themes such as identity, race, and class, getting her voice—and that of women—heard. *The Inspiring Women Frida Kahlo Barbie* celebrates the revolutionary achievements, heroism, and enduring contributions that Frida made to the world of art and to women. Her life and her extraordinary art continue to influence and inspire others to follow their dreams and envision their own realities.

2023

# The Barbie Movie

**SIGNIFICANCE:** FROM DOLLS TO HUMAN AND BACK!

Barbiemania reached a new peak in 2023 with the release of the movie, *Barbie,* directed by Greta Gerwig, which became an instant classic. On the big screen, Margot Robbie starred as Barbie, while Ryan Gosling played Ken. In the movie, Barbie's world became a vehicle for reinterpreting many of the social and aesthetic phenomena from the second half of the 20th and the early 21st centuries—including art, history, society, lifestyles, and fashion. Closely resembling their Mattel counterparts, the two actors were transformed into Barbie and Ken, complete with signature makeup and some of their most iconic outfits. For example, in the movie's trailer, Margot Robbie wore the look of the first Barbie from 1959, and in the

## 2023

opening scenes she wore the pink gingham dress from the 1964 *Swirl Ponytail* doll. When she and Ken first stepped into the real world, they both wore outfits that echoed the Western line from 1980. Later, when they skated along the boardwalk, they wore a look inspired by *Barbie Hot Skating* from 1994. This blending of past and present continued on the red carpet: at premieres around the world, Margot Robbie wore looks inspired by Barbie's best-known outfits. With the help of big fashion houses like Vivienne Westwood, Schiaparelli, Versace, Hervé Leger and Pucci, it was possible to recreate looks such as *Solo in the Spotlight* and *Enchanted Evening* (1960), *Black Magic* (1963), *Day-to-Night* (1985), and *Totally Hair* (1991). The two *Barbie* movie commemorative dolls featured Robbie's Barbie in a pink gingham dress and Gosling's Ken in his pastel blue-and-cream striped beachwear. From dolls to humans, and back again!

## 2024

# Barbie 65th Anniversary

No one would ever believe it, but on March 9, 2024, Barbie celebrated her 65th anniversary. A milestone such as this had to be celebrated in grand style—and, of course, a look that lived up to a lifelong legacy of success, innovation, creativity, and inspiration. To commemorate Barbie's 65th anniversary, Mattel created two collectible Barbie dolls that honored to the doll's history. Wearing matching outfits they paid tribute to her black-and-white debut look, reimagined for the future in grand gala style: a scalloped ballgown with a bodice and sweetheart neckline, transparent petticoat, and long black gloves.

## 2024

Completing the look and tribute were sapphire-hued earrings—the 65th anniversary color—and cat-eye sunglasses with light blue lenses. The makeup was based on that of the first model of the doll, while the hairstyle, with a cascade of wavy hair, was modern and timeless ... just like Barbie.

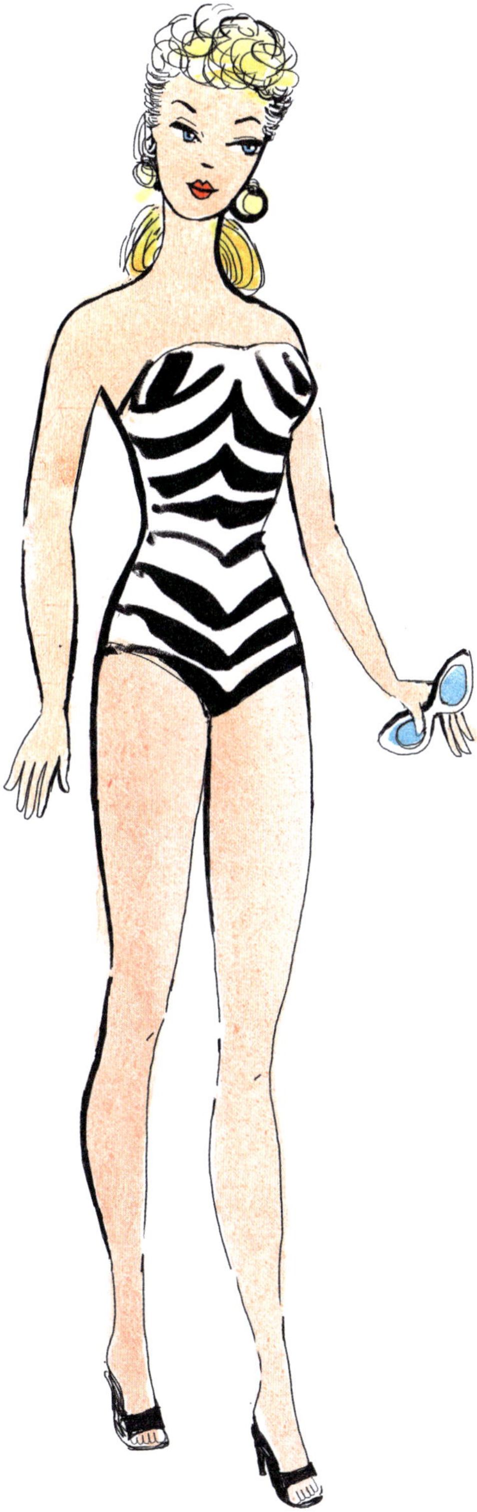

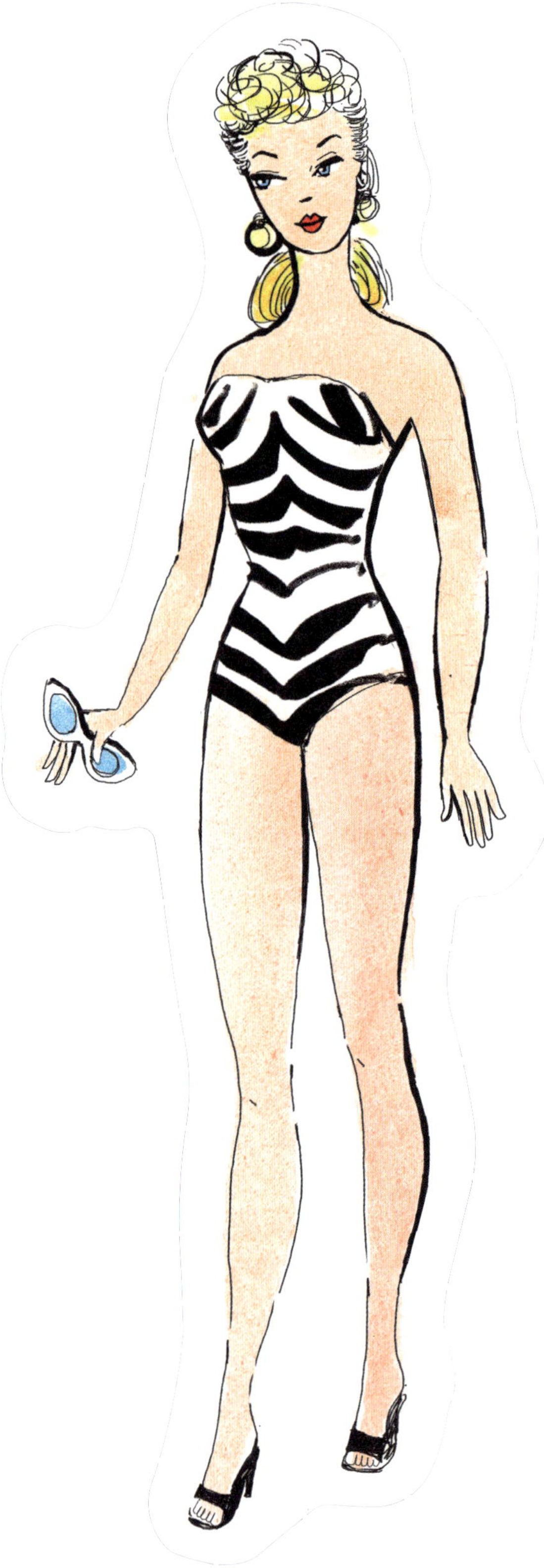